# Contents

Ron Matheson

**2** Quips & Quotes

**4** Planet of the Apes

America's Sweethearts **8**

**12** Captain Corelli's Mandolin

*All-American Series:*
**American Graffiti, American Pie and American Pie 2**

**18**

**23** Video Illustrations

*Classic Movie*
**The Graduate** **27**

**31** Point/Counterpoint

Use REEL FAITH in Creative Settings **33**

# Quips & Quotes

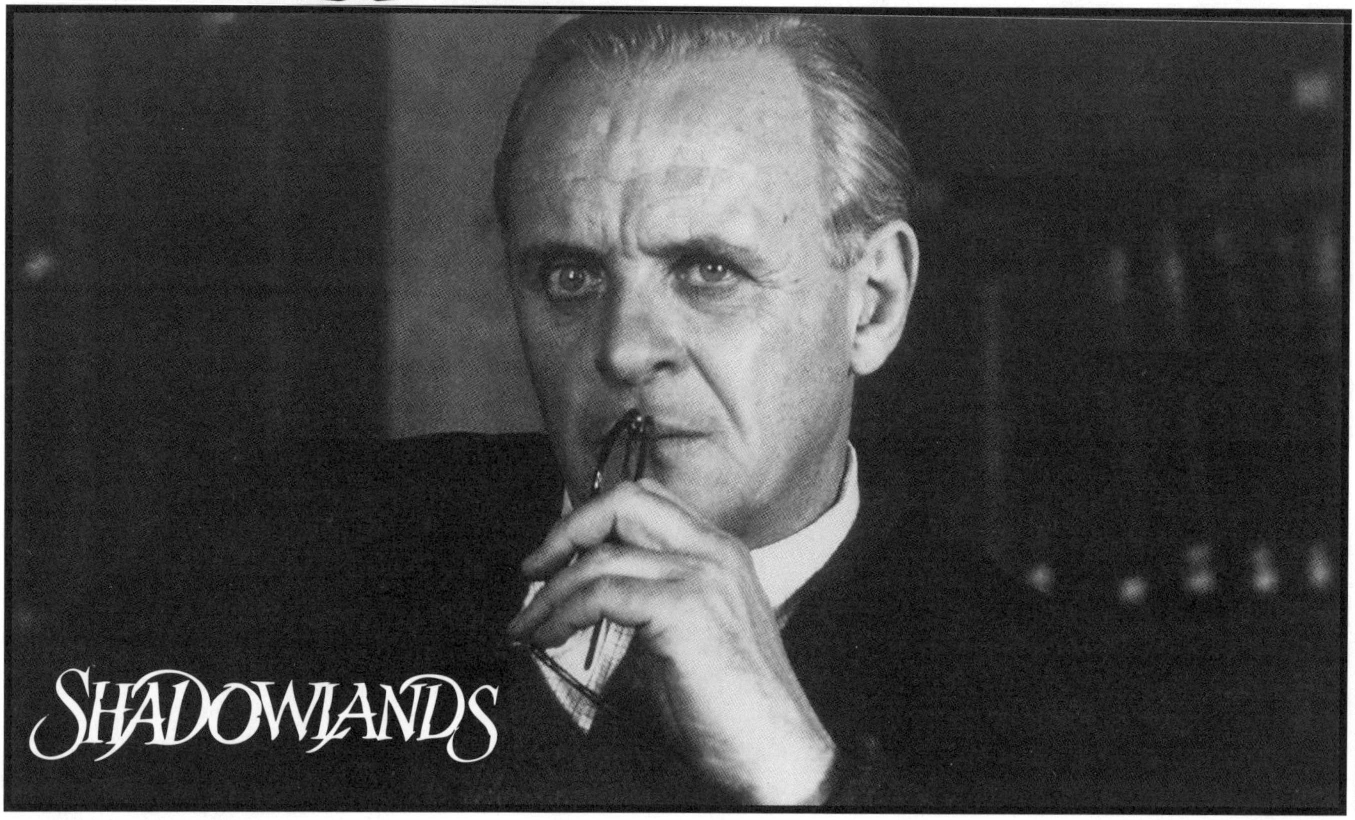

### SHADOWLANDS

Man is not truly one but truly two. Good and bad carry on an eternal struggle. If these two selves could be separated, the evil could be liberated.
—Fredric March as Dr. Jekyll in *Dr. Jekyll and Mr. Hyde* (1931)
**Romans 7:15-21**

I have to believe in a world outside my own mind. I have to believe that my actions still have meaning ... even if I can't remember them. I have to believe that when my eyes are closed, the world's still there.
—Guy Pearce as Leonard Shelby in *Memento* (2000)
**2 Corinthians 4:16—5:7**

The pathway to salvation is as narrow and as difficult to walk as a razor's edge.
—A Tibetan monk speaking to Larry Darrell (Bill Murray) in *The Razor's Edge* (1984)
**Matthew 7:13-14**

No man can ever hope to know the real nature of God, but he has given us a glimpse of his face.
—Raymond Massey as the prophet Nathan in *David and Bathsheba* (1951)
**Philippians 2:5-11**

Vice? Virtue? It's best not to be too moral. You cheat yourself out of too much life. Aim above morality. As Confucius says, "Don't simply be good; make good things happen."
—Ruth Gordon as Maude in *Harold and Maude* (1971)
**Luke 6:43-45**

HARRY: Christopher can scoff, Jack, but I know how hard you've been praying; and now God is answering your prayers.
C. S. LEWIS: That's not why I pray, Harry. I pray because I can't help myself. I pray because I'm helpless. I pray because the need flows out of me all the time, waking and sleeping. Prayer doesn't change God, it changes me.
—Exchange between C. S. Lewis (Anthony Hopkins) and his friend "Harry" Harrington (Michael Denison) in *Shadowlands* (1993)
**Luke 11:1-4, Ephesians 6:18**

REEL FAITH

GHANDI: Doesn't the New Testament say, "If your enemy strikes you on the right cheek, offer him your left?"

REV. CHARLIE ANDREWS: I think perhaps the phrase was used metaphorically.

GHANDI: I'm not so sure. I have thought about it a great deal, and I suspect he meant you must show courage. Be willing to take a blow—several blows—to show that you will not strike back nor will you be turned aside. And when you do that it calls upon something in human nature, something that makes his hatred for you decrease and his respect increase. I think Christ grasped that, and I have seen it work.

—Gandhi (Ben Kingsley) in an exchange with the Reverend Charlie Andrews (Ian Charleson) in *Gandhi* (1982)

**Matthew 5:38-46**

There's an old joke. Uh, two elderly women are at a Catskills mountain resort, and one of 'em says, "Boy, the food at this place is really terrible." The other one says, "Yeah, I know, and such small portions." Well, that's essentially how I feel about life. Full of loneliness and misery and suffering and unhappiness, and it's all over much too quickly.

—Woody Allen as Alvy Singer in *Annie Hall* (1977)

**2 Corinthians 1:3-7**

## Top Ten Portrayals of Satan

Sometimes you can learn something new about the nature of God by watching God's adversary at work. Hollywood has always had a fascination with Satan. Here is our list of Satan's top ten appearances in the movies. If you think we've left off of our list an obvious or important portrayal of Satan, write us at Bob Shell, 201 Eighth Avenue South, Nashville, TN, 37203 or email us at youth@abingdonpress.com and we'll print your additions in a future issue.

1. Al Pacino in *The Devil's Advocate* (1997)
2. Jack Nicholson in *The Witches of Eastwick* (1987)
3. Billy Crystal in *Deconstructing Harry* (1997)
4. Tim Curry in *Legend* (1985)
5. Robert De Niro in *Angel Heart* (1987)
6. Bill Cosby in *The Devil and Max Devlin* (1981)
7. Gabriel Byrne in *End of Days* (1999)
8. Gustav Berger II in *God, Man and Devil* (1950)
9. George Burns in *Oh, God! You Devil* (1984)
10. Elizabeth Hurley/Peter Cook in *Bedazzled* (2000, 1967)

# PLANET OF THE APES

## Background
*Planet of the Apes* (1968) is 112 minutes long and is rated G. *Planet of the Apes* (2001) is 119 minutes and rated PG-13 for some sequences of action/violence.

## Cautions
*Planet of the Apes* (2001) is rated PG-13 for some sequences of action and violence.

## Academy Awards
*Planet of the Apes* (1968) was nominated for two Oscars: Best Costume Design and Best Music, Original Score for a Motion Picture (not a musical).

> He also told this parable to some who trusted in themselves that they were righteous and regarded others with contempt: "Two men went up to the temple to pray, one a Pharisee and the other a tax collector. The Pharisee, standing by himself, was praying thus, 'God, I thank you that I am not like other people: thieves, rogues, adulterers, or even like this tax collector. I fast twice a week; I give a tenth of all my income.' But the tax collector, standing far off, would not even look up to heaven, but was beating his breast and saying, 'God, be merciful to me, a sinner!' I tell you, this man went down to his home justified rather than the other; for all who exalt themselves will be humbled, but all who humble themselves will be exalted."
> (Luke 18:9-14)

A seminarian and the late Dr. Earl D. C. Brewer were traveling through the Kentucky countryside. After a particularly long silence, Dr. Brewer asked, "Do you read science fiction?" The student eventually replied, "Yes." Another long silence followed. Dr. Brewer asked, "How often do you read science fiction?" The student replied, "Sometimes several books a week." Dr. Brewer said, "Good." The student mumbled in a low voice, "Why do you want to know?" Dr. Brewer said, "Because people who are interested in changing the world read science fiction. A person has to have the ability to imagine other than what they see in order to change society and the world around them. Science fiction is good practice for the real thing." Pierre Boulle certainly conceived of a world different than our own with the book *La Planete Des Singes* (*Planet of the Apes*). In his original novel, a wealthy couple leisurely travels between star systems by solar sail. In the emptiness they find a bottle containing a manuscript. They open it and read the autobiography of a man named Ulysee Mérou, an astronaut, who explores the system of Betelgeuse. He discovers a world similar to Earth in which apes are intelligent and humans irrational and incapable of speech. Eventually, the man returns to Earth and upon landing is greeted by a gorilla. The couple is shocked by the story. They are chimpanzees!

Boulle wrote the novel *La Planete Des Singes* in 1963, first translated with the name *Monkey Planet*. Boulle, a native of France, trained as an engineer and went to work on a rubber plantation in Malaysia. Caught by World War II, he became a secret agent for Allied France, was captured by the Japanese, and after two years as a prisoner of war, escaped. Another of his novels, *Bridge Over the River Kwai* (*Le Pont De La Riviere Kwai*), was published in 1952, adapted for film in 1957, and won the Academy Award for Best Picture. The screenplay for *Planet of the Apes*, written in 1968, was followed by a number of film sequels, books, and other spinoffs—none written by Boulle but based on his conception. Another of Boulle's publications, *Time Out of Mind*, a noteworthy book of science fiction short stories, was a bestseller. Boulle died at age eighty-one in 1994 but continued to write almost until the time of his death. One of his final works was about the industrial commercialization and exploitation of persons with HIV and AIDS.

The vision of Pierre Boulle's searing wartime experience, particularly as a POW, provides the foundation for both *Bridge On the River Kwai* and *Planet of the Apes*. That vision forcefully continues in the following adapted screenplays, novels, and television shows, even though other people wrote them. The relationship between the Allied prisoners and Japanese soldiers found in *Bridge On the River Kwai* shifts to men and animals in *Planet of the Apes*. Both books/screenplays illustrate that the devastation of weaker groups repressed by stronger groups results in moral consequences for both groups.

## Discussing and Learning

➤ What signs do the humans exhibit in *Planet of the Apes* 2001 that are the result of repression? (*poverty, fearfulness, hopelessness, lack of education*)

➤ What are examples of ideologically driven behavior in *Planet of the Apes* 2001? (*General Thad's and his father's actions, the prejudice by the educated apes against humans*)

➤ How are Thad's beliefs and behaviors somewhat grounded in history? (*Apes were originally used like trained lab mice for space exploration and were therefore exploited.*)

➤ What happens to the civilian government in *Planet of the Apes* 2001 when a perceived crisis occurs? (*The military takes over for anti-democratic use of power.*)

➤ Are there other examples in *Planet of the Apes* 2001 of Pierre Boulle's wartime experiences? (*prisoners of war, slavery, medical experiments*)

The *Planet of the Apes* 1968 screenplay by Rod Serling (*The Twilight Zone*) and Michael Wilson (black listed by the Committee on Un-American Activities) takes a somewhat different tack than Boulle's novel. Humans are intelligent, but apes dominate. Astronauts travel intentionally to near light speed on a one-way relativistic trip to the future. They overshoot their time goal and arrive a good bit later than planned. At the end the main character, played by Charlton Heston, learns he has returned to his own world but after a nuclear holocaust.

*Planet of the Apes* 2001, directed by Tim Burton, uses the convention of an electromagnetic time storm, thrusting the main character (actor Mark Wahlberg) far into the future. He crash lands on a planet where humans are intelligent and used as slaves or as subjects of medical experiments by the predominant apes. He eventually learns that his mother ship, by quirk of the storm, arrived hundreds of years earlier and its inhabitants, ape and human, are descendants of his former crewmates.

In the grand spirit of authors H. G. Wells, Aldous Huxley, and Jules Verne, the *Planet of the Apes* series uses science fiction to: (1) think about what could be, (2) consider ethical consequences of future

REEL FAITH 5

possible technical advances, and (3) question our society as it is in the present. Questions about fascism and totalitarianism, species equality, and military buildup are raised throughout the *Planet of the Apes* series. Consequences of technological advancement appear in *Planet of the Apes* 2001.

➤ Jumping from the present to the future and back, by accident or intention, may never happen. But what about genetic enhancement? If we have the power to genetically enhance other species, should we follow through?

Big science news reveals that the human genome is now mapped. Genetic manipulation of plants and animals already is taking place. Like it or not, much of the United States population has already eaten gene-enhanced corn that produces pesticide pollen or tomatoes with antifreeze genes. In *Planet of the Apes* 2001, the apes on the ship are part of genetic experiments to enhance intelligence.

➤ Do you feel human beings should experiment this way? Are

COPYRIGHT © 2001 TWENTIETH CENTURY FOX (ALL RIGHTS RESERVED).

such experiments necessary in order to create a better world for future generations? What is our loving responsibility to the future generations?

➤ Are we committing the sin of pride when we begin to manipulate genes? (*Consider historic government reaction to people like Galileo and Copernicus.*)

➤ Should the Wright brothers have foreseen the negative consequences of flight? (*Some negative consequences may be the fire bombing of Dresden, the World Trade Centers, Hiroshima*)

➤ In the parable of the Pharisee and the tax collector, the tax collector recognizes himself to be a sinner and asks, even demands, that God be merciful to him. We usually read this story, thank God we are not like the Pharisee, and thus become the Pharisee. What present cultural or societal behavior does *Planet of the Apes* question? (*Ethics relating to animals, extreme ideological behavior, militarism*)

➤ Discuss the way in which the parable of the Pharisee and the tax collector breaks down any distinctions that one class or type of person is "better" than another. How is this reflected in *Planet of the Apes*?

The nineteenth-century German scientist, Paul Brocca, discovered that one particular part of the human brain controls the ability to speak. Named in his honor, Brocca's region of the human brain is not found in other primates. When this section of the brain is damaged through accident or disease, a person loses the ability to speak, yet he or she often is able to think and comprehend. Another area of the cerebral cortex, called Wenicke's area (also named after its discoverer), seems to control understanding and comprehension. When Wenicke's area is damaged, a person may be able to speak but without comprehension. Though today it is not technically possible nor feasible due to the incredible complexity of determining the specific genes, future scientists might be able to splice the genes that are responsible for the human Brocca's or Wenicke's regions into other primates.

➤ What would be the ethical consequences of such action?

➤ Do you think primates enhanced in Brocca's region and Wenicke's area would be given legal protective rights?

➤ Would these new creatures have souls and a relationship to God? The apes in *Planet of the Apes* believe that they have souls while humans do not. What do you think about this reversal?

➤ Would current slavery laws apply to these beings as possible future workers or warriors?

➤ On his Internet site (*www.biotechcentury.org/rifkin.html*), Jeremy Rifkin warns about the current simple genetic manipulation of crops. Brainstorm with your group about possible unforeseen consequences of genetic enhancement for plants and animals.

Speculative science fiction provides ample opportunity to consider the "what ifs" of future human and technical development. *The Island of Dr. Moreau* by H. G. Wells (and subsequent movies) as well as *20,000 Leagues Under the Sea* and other books by Jules Verne (and their movie screenplays) were scoffed as delusional when they first appeared. However, today, air flight, submarines, trips to the moon and other planets, machines that seem to think, and genetic engineering are common place. Yet all were first conceptualized in science fiction. The current *Brightleaf* series of science fiction books offers the following for consideration: Benevolent intelligence enhancement of one species by another already intelligent species is necessary to the maturation of both species and future culture.

➤ Historically, once a technical advancement is made or discovered, it continues though its advancement may be slowed. For example, silk culture, fire, use of energy, the wheel, internal combustion, flight, agriculture, gun powder, the telephone, genetic manipulation, and other scientific methods leading to various principles and theories all continue in various forms. How should Christians approach technological advances? Should technical intelligence enhancement of another species be approached as nurture? Did the original apes in the 2001 version revolt because they were being used as slaves?

The apes in Planet of the Apes 2001, Frankenstein, the character Data from Star Trek: The Next Generation, and the computer HAL in 2001: A Space Odyssey share a common link. In each story a being, series of beings, or some type of intelligence is created by someone other than God. These entities can follow directions, think, and act but if left unattended may cause a great deal of trouble. Medieval Jewish folklore tells the tale(s) of the golem. The word golem derives from a Hebrew word that means "formless or shapeless." In most of the traditional stories, a golem that looks like a man but is not a man is created after elaborate ritual; and then, after running amuck, the rabbi/creator must destroy the golem. HAL had to be destroyed. Data was afforded the rights of a human. The intelligent apes in Planet of the Apes 2001 developed their own culture.

➤ Consider doing an Internet search for the word *golem*. Current conceptions of golems range from self-replicating robots or computers to various types of biological genetic manipulation that includes cloning.

➤ Do you think it is possible for an artificial intelligence like Data on *Star Trek* or a genetically enhanced primate like those in *Planet of the Apes* 2001 to eventually be considered as a person? Is artificial life actually life? What defines *personhood*?

➤ A serious early response to the question, *Is human flight possible?*, was that God would have given us wings if God had intended humans to fly. Just as humans learned to fly, humans will learn to manipulate genetics. Should we argue that if God had intended other species to possess enhanced intelligence, God would have given it to them? How do you feel about the preceding statement?

➤ Do we have the right to manipulate genes? The United States government has decreed that cloning is illegal and unethical. What do you think? Do you think cloning and other genetic manipulation will eventually be successfully controlled? What would be the Christian, loving, ethical approach to creation of other intelligent life? (as a loving parent?)

In *Planet of the Apes* 2001 Leo Davidson is more impulsive than self-reflective (unlike Taylor in the original). He realizes his ship and shipmates could well have landed on the new planet because he disobeyed orders and dashed after his pet. When Leo does show remorse he seems to be more concerned with himself than others.

Though he does aid in changing ape and human relationships, he abandons his new friends and rushes back to Earth. Other than aiding the humans during the battle scene, the view is left wondering if he behaves as a trained military officer at any time. The 2001 ending, though shocking, does not pack the punch of Taylor's emotional and spiritual agony upon discovering civilization wiped out by nuclear holocaust. The 2001 ending merely presents the audience with a big "oops." However, even in the current *Planet of the Apes*, Pierre Boulle's social concerns with societal abuse remain.

➤ What does it mean to treat animals ethically and humanely? (You may want to view the movie *Instinct* as a followup to *Planet of the Apes*.)

➤ What was Leo's ethical responsibility to the apes and humans on the new planet? As the one trained and educated person on the new planet, should he have tried to return to Earth?

➤ On a fairly deep level, *Planet of the Apes* asks, "Who are you?" Discuss the answer to that question, as well as, are you a sinner in need of God's mercy?

➤ Will we create a race of slaves by manipulating genes?

➤ Are we capable of nurturing new biological forms or artificial intelligences to maturity in understanding?

➤ Read the second chapter of Genesis. How does the story of Adam and Eve relate to the story told in *Planet of the Apes* 2001? (Remember, the new apes develop their own individual wills.)

REEL FAITH 7

# America's Sweethearts

Eddie Thomas and Gwen Harrison were a hot couple in Hollywood. They made nine movies together before their marriage fell apart. Gwen cheated on Eddie with a Spaniard named Hector, a dimwitted guy with a purposefully bad Spanish accent played by Hank Azaria. The time has come to promote the last movie Eddie and Gwen made together, *Time Over Time*. Publicist Lee Phillips' task is to convince the two to do a media junket to generate box-office interest in their film. Neither wants to have anything to do with the other, but Lee and Kiki, Gwen's sister and assistant, eventually manage to talk Gwen and Eddie into promoting the film.

Matters are complicated by the eccentric director, Hal Weidmann, who refuses to allow anyone at the studio or in the media an advance viewing of the film. Lee must perpetuate a bluffing game for the media and empty praise for the two stars, or the whole thing will fall apart. Fittingly, the junket is held in a hotel in the middle of the Nevada desert—chosen by Lee so the media have nowhere to go when they realize he doesn't actually have the film.

The five-minute junket interviews begin with different reporters repeatedly asking the same type of questions in a grueling day-long push. Afterward Lee schemes again to arrange a dinner with Eddie and Gwen in an attempt to generate rumors of a reconciliation. Eventually Gwen does arrive for dinner in a red-sequined dress designed to show up Kiki, who secretly has been in love with Eddie for a long time. Kiki leaves Eddie and Gwen in the restaurant just as Hector shows up unexpectedly. Hector picks a fight with Eddie who ends up with a big cut to his left eye. Kiki nurses his wound with an ice pack, and finally they kiss. But the next morning as soon as Gwen calls, Eddie runs to her. Exasperated, Kiki tells Eddie the truth: Gwen only came on the junket to salvage her career and give Eddie the divorce papers.

## Background

*America's Sweethearts* is 102 minutes long and is rated PG-13.

## Cautions

*America's Sweethearts* is rated PG-13 for language, brief nudity, and sexual innuendo.

> Do not give what is holy to dogs; and do not throw your pearls before swine, or they will trample them under foot and turn and maul you.
> (Matthew 7:6)
>
> . . . Whatever is true, whatever is honorable, whatever is just, whatever is pure, whatever is pleasing, whatever is commendable, if there is any excellence and if there is anything worthy of praise, think about these things.
> (Philippians 4:8)

When the movie finally premieres, it becomes obvious that the eccentric director has produced a behind-the-scenes exposé of Hollywood, revealing both the backstabbing and the obsequious praise. Gwen is furious, and in front of all the press, threatens a lawsuit against the director. When she realizes she is coming across to the media as a shrew, she immediately tries to reverse her behavior and sweetly manipulate Eddie into announcing their reconciliation. Eddie, who finally has developed a backbone, explains that all this time he has been in love with the person Gwen portrays on the screen, not who she is in real life. He then proclaims his love for Kiki, Kiki gracefully stands up to her sister Gwen, and together Kiki and Eddie leave the junket. Lee, being a publicist, is thrilled at the press attention this change in events provides *Time Over Time*.

## Discussing and Learning

### What Really Matters in Relationships

*America's Sweethearts* raises some interesting questions about the foundation of relationships between men and women: what to look for in a mate, how to build a solid marriage, and the need for boundaries to prevent manipulation by selfish people. The discussion starters below explore these issues and relate them to three different Bible passages.

♥ Describe Gwen. (*Gwen is the epitome of selfishness. She sees everything in terms of how it affects her and behaves terribly with her sister Kiki. Yet the public always perceives Gwen as sweet.*)

♥ What do you think of Gwen's marriage with Eddie? (*Eddie probably worshiped the ground Gwen walked on, always at her beck and call, trying to please her.*)

♥ Why would such a relationship create an atmosphere for failure? (*It's an unbalanced relationship, with one person primarily taking and the other primarily giving. The giver usually ends up exhausted and unhappy. Relationships work best when both partners give 100 percent—their very best to each other. Even a 50/50 or 60/40 split creates an atmosphere in which each partner is keeping score.*

> "How can you be in love with someone and not even like them at the same time?"
> —Eddie talks to Kiki about his relationship with Gwen

*Another reason the relationship would fail is that a demanding partner like Gwen tends to be fickle, impatient, and immature. When hard times come or romantic feelings fade, that type person quickly looks for a way out of the commitment, as Gwen did in her affair with Hector.*)

♥ Gwen and Eddie are good examples of how not to build a relationship. Read Matthew 7:24-27. In these verses Jesus speaks about building our individual lives on the strong foundation of believing in God and living out Jesus' teachings in our daily lives. Married believers not only need to follow Jesus individually, but they also need to put Christ at the center of their marriage relationship. Eddie and Gwen's marriage was built on the sinking sand of selfishness and worldly values. What practical things can we do to build our relationships on the rock of Christ? (*In addition*

REEL FAITH

to spending time individually fostering each person's spiritual growth, couples need to spend regular time together praying, studying God's Word, and discussing insights God gives each partner. Worshiping with other believers each week is important. Participating in a small group Bible study challenges couples to grow, provides direction in personal Bible study, and gives the rich support of Christian friendship and prayer that is necessary for relationships to thrive.)

♥ What made Kiki so appealing, and why were she and Eddie well-suited for each other? (*Kiki remained kind, caring, patient, and down-to-earth in an industry full of self-important people. They shared a camaraderie strengthened by enduring Gwen's diva moments. They attempted to be truthful with each other, and eventually, neither put his or her own needs above the other person's needs. Each possessed similar positive character traits but different personalities—a nice mix to keep life interesting. For example, Eddie was less organized and more spontaneous than Kiki.*)

> "So, what you're really worried about is you."
> —Kiki to Gwen when Kiki is trying to convince Gwen to do the junket. Later Gwen says this to Kiki when Kiki asserts her independence from Gwen.

♥ What do you look for in a mate? Read Philippians 2:1-8 for the antithesis of Gwen and typical Hollywood attitudes about important factors in relationships. Discuss the traits of Jesus that Paul encourages us to imitate and how those traits can be particularly helpful in marriage.

♥ Read Matthew 7:6. How does Jesus' advice apply to Eddie and Kiki in this movie? (*Kiki was wasting her generous, serving heart on a sister who would never really respect or appreciate her. In Eddie's marriage to Gwen, he lavished his love on a selfish, manipulative woman. He hung on even after she was unfaithful. Neither Kiki nor Eddie needed to burn every bridge with Gwen, but both needed to set appropriate boundaries in their relationships with Gwen. They began this process during the public confrontation at the movie's premiere [1:30]*).

### Behind the Glitz and Glamour: Hollywood's Artificiality

The entire movie pokes fun at the artificiality of everyone and everything in Hollywood, from Gwen's two-faced persona to the cut-throat publicist Lee Phillips, to the eccentric director of *Time Over Time* who turned Eddie and Gwen's final movie together into a exposé of Hollywood. Except for Eddie and Kiki, everyone is scheming everyone in this movie.

♥ What do the average American man and woman look like? Compare that description with the typical movie actor and actress. What does this tell you about Hollywood's artificiality?

♥ Ask the group to recall from the movie as many examples as possible that depict the artificial nature of Hollywood. Include some of the following in your discussion:
1. Eddie's New Age guru (:17)
2. Lee the publicist runs back and forth between limousines to negotiate Eddie and Gwen's arrival at the junket (:27).

3. Eddie and Gwen put on their game faces for the photographers when first arriving at the junket (:29).
4. Lee the publicist leaks the so-called masturbation scene to the press and barely saves Eddie from falling off the roof—all to gain press attention for *Time Over Time* (:38, 1:18).
5. Eddie and Gwen plan several lies to answer the expected media questions about their relationship (:45).
6. Eddie and Gwen repeatedly answer the same questions in each five-minute interview, as if they have never been asked the questions before (:49).

10 REEL FAITH

7. Hal Weidmann, the eccentric director, creates the behind-the-scenes exposé film, which reveals that everyone is talking behind everyone else's back (1:23).
8. Gwen's diva nature portrays her as sweet on camera but nasty and rude off camera (1:26).
9. Eddie announces in front of the press that he had been in love with the person Gwen portrays on screen, not who she was in real life (1:30).
10. The title of the movie-within-the-movie, *Time Over Time*, evokes the idea of the same story being released again and again—nothing fresh tends to come out of Hollywood.
11. Julia Roberts wore a fat suit during the scenes in which she was supposed to appear sixty pounds heavier; note that Kiki received romantic male attention only after she lost the weight.

"I am done pretending that your life is my whole life."
—Kiki to Gwen

♥ How do movies produced in or about Hollywood tend to influence us? *(Answers may include fashion, our perceptions of physical beauty such as anorexic women, breast implants, botox-filled lips, and so on, the idealization of extramarital sex glamorized in unrealistic as well as non-biblical ways.)*

♥ Read Philippians 4:8-9. On a large sheet of paper, list the qualities in verse 8 that God values, and ask the group to brainstorm examples of each. Then ask, "How do movies, television, and popular magazines stack up to these criteria?"

♥ What attitudes do you possess that are influenced more by Hollywood than by God's values? Read Romans 12:2. What changes do you need the Holy Spirit to make in your life so that you have realistic expectations and view people through God's eyes?

## Superstar Password

Before the session, write each name below on an index card. Divide the group into pairs or teams of five, and assign one person to give the clues (five actor or actress names per round). The purpose is to guess the actor or actress. No gestures are allowed, and in the final round, limit the clues to one word at a time. Complete one category at a time and clearly announce the category. The cluegiver may pass on one item per round. Limit time to approximately two minutes per round. Consider a final round that features the pair or team with the most points from previous rounds.

**Classic Actresses**
Greta Garbo, Ingrid Bergman, Katharine Hepburn, Audrey Hepburn, Marilyn Monroe, Shirley Temple, Jean Harlow, Joan Crawford, Elizabeth Taylor, Olivia de Havilland, Bette Davis, Sophia Loren, Lucille Ball

**Classic Actors**
Clark Gable, Humphrey Bogart, Cary Grant, Gregory Peck, Sidney Poitier, Errol Flynn, Jose Ferrer, Gary Cooper, James Stewart, John Wayne, James Mason, Kirk Douglas, Laurence Olivier, Paul Newman

**Contemporary Actresses**
Julia Roberts, Sally Fields, Helen Hunt, Meryl Streep, Julie Andrews, Vivica A. Fox, Jennifer Lopez, Shirley MacLaine, Jodie Foster, Charlize Theron, Meg Ryan, Catherine Zeta-Jones, Drew Barrymore, Sandra Bullock, Gwyneth Paltrow

**Contemporary Actors**
Robert Redford, Will Smith, Robert De Niro, Denzel Washington, Jackie Chan, Harrison Ford, Tom Hanks, Sean Connery, Tommy Lee Jones, Matthew McConaughey, Mel Gibson, Tom Cruise, Bruce Willis, Michael Caine, Eddie Murphy, Matt Damon, Ben Affleck, Richard Gere, Danny Glover

REEL FAITH  11

# Captain Corelli's Mandolin

"You have heard that it was said, 'An eye for an eye and a tooth for a tooth.' But I say to you, Do not resist an evildoer. But if anyone strikes you on the right cheek, turn the other also; and if anyone wants to sue you and take your coat, give your cloak as well; and if anyone forces you to go one mile, go also the second mile."
(Matthew 5:38-41)

"You have heard that it was said, 'You shall love your neighbor and hate your enemy.' But I say to you, Love your enemies and pray for those who persecute you, so that you may be children of your Father in heaven; for he makes his sun rise on the evil and on the good, and sends rain on the righteous and on the unrighteous. For if you love those who love you, what reward do you have? Do not even the tax collectors do the same? And if you greet only your brothers and sisters, what more are you doing than others? Do not even the Gentiles do the same? Be perfect, therefore, as your heavenly Father is perfect."
(Matthew 5:43-48)

## Finding Love in the Midst of Conflict

*Captain Corelli's Mandolin* provides a perfect springboard to discuss ways to find love in the midst of conflict. It begins with a humorous episode in which Dr. Iannis removes an ancient pea from the ear of old Stamatis, healing his lifelong deafness. The old man's wife, suddenly aware that he no longer has an excuse for ignoring her, begins to make up for lost time by releasing the complaints pent up for decades of marriage. By the end of the movie, Stamatis is begging Dr. Iannis to replace the pea. While these scenes, carefully placed at the beginning and the end of the movie, may seem to be only comic backdrops for the more important story in between, they are actually the story itself in microcosm. Dr. Iannis refuses to replace the pea; instead he instructs Stamatis to search for love in his marriage, even in the midst of the torturous nagging.

When Italian Captain Antonio Corelli and his men land on the Greek island of Cephallonia, it is clear they would rather enjoy life than

### Background
*Captain Corelli's Mandolin* is rated R and is 127 minutes long.

### Cautions
This movie is rated R for sexuality, language, and war-related violence.

12  REEL FAITH

make war. Like many of their real-life counterparts (see "The Real Story Behind Captain Corelli's Mandolin" on page 16), Corelli and his men are not followers of Mussolini's Fascism. Caught between a dictator's evil and their natural desire to live peaceful, happy lives, Corelli's men treat Cephallonia like a vacation paradise while drinking wine, enjoying women, and singing opera choruses. They are unwilling victors making the best of a bad situation.

The Greeks, understandably, resent the occupation. No matter how benevolent the men of Acqui Division, the inescapable reality is that they are the enemy. Freedom is restricted. The situation comes to a head when the Italian officers are billeted in Greek homes without the consent of the owners. This is how Antonio Corelli meets Pelagia Iannis, the doctor's daughter. Pelagia's sense of justice is severely tested when she must cook and clean for the enemy. And although Corelli volunteers to sleep in the yard, Pelagia stubbornly refuses to find anything admirable about him. He is, after all, the enemy, and she knows she is supposed to hate her enemies.

Jesus faced the same situation in the first century. Palestine was occupied by the Romans (Italians), and few citizens were happy about it. For the most part, the Romans were peaceful victors. As long as a defeated country refrained from open revolt, Rome allowed its people a remarkable amount of freedom. Nevertheless, indignities occurred. It was legal, for instance, for a Roman soldier to command a citizen of an occupied country to carry his equipment a certain distance. Also, Rome often taxed the citizens of these countries beyond their ability to pay. The residents of Palestine did not have to look far for a reason to hate their enemies, the Romans.

Yet Jesus said, "Love your enemies." Many scholars believe that when he uttered those words he was referring specifically to the Romans. Rome was almost certainly the focus of Matthew 5:41: "If anyone forces you to go one mile, go also the second mile." He was referring to the Roman soldiers' practice of forcing the people to carry their equipment.

Jesus understood the futility of war with the superpower of his day. But he understood something more important: Teaching his followers to love their enemies was not a weakling's withdrawal from conflict. Instead, it was resistance to the powers of evil. Some call it passive resistance. Nevertheless, it is a form of action, in that it actively redefines power and reassigns the position of power to the one who is being oppressed.

When Antonio Corelli plays his mandolin for Pelagia, he participates in an overture of love that spans the ages. The mandolin, an ancient instrument historically associated with the music of love, sings a sweet song that few can resist. It becomes a symbol of the common bond of love, even in the midst of conflict. Once Pelagia sets aside her conception of the way things should be and allows herself to see the enemy as a human being, love gains a foothold.

Love is stronger than war and stronger than hatred, but it needs a place to grow. As Christians, that is where we come in. We are called to look for the humanity in people with whom we are in conflict. Whether those persons are to be found in work relationships, friendships, families, marriages, or even in warring nations, Jesus' command is clear: "Love your enemy." He calls for personal sacrifice and for our attention to be focused upon the enemy instead of our own needs. He does not call for abandonment to evil (see "Discussing and Learning"), but he does call for our willingness to give love a place to grow as Jesus own words tell us: "For if you love those who love you, what reward do you have? Do not even the tax collectors do the same? And if you greet only your brothers and sisters, what more are you doing than others?" (Matthew 5:46-47).

## Discussing and Learning

**What Does It Mean to Love Our Enemies?**

Begin by reading aloud Matthew 5:38-41, 43-48. Allow time for persons to react before discussing the questions below. Some may question the command to love our enemies. Encourage free expression of thoughts and explain that the discussion questions focus on the ideas presented in this Scripture.

🎸 Watch the first four minutes of the movie that feature the voice of Dr. Iannis saying: "I promised Pelagia I would write a history ... to understand why the gods bless us or shake us. I wanted her to not ask why we are wounded, only if we can be healed." How do Dr. Iannis' words reflect Jesus' own thoughts in the Scripture? (*Jesus' words are remarkable in that they change the point of focus for those who are oppressed. Instead of focusing on our wounds—be they literal or spiritual—Jesus wants us to focus on the one who has wounded us. Doing this helps us to break the cycle of hatred and points us to the process of healing.*)

🎸 Watch the scene when Dr. Iannis tries to convince Pelagia not to marry Mandras (0:09). At the end of the conversation he hands her a gun, saying, "There is going to be a war. Marriage will have to wait." He gives her the gun because he fears the occupying forces will commit atrocities, including raping the women of the island. This brings up the issue of self-defense. How can we love our enemies as Jesus has commanded and still protect ourselves from harm? (*It is often dangerous to apply broad principles to specific situations. That type application is called casuistry. A casuist is usually considered an unreasonable thinker, because broad principles rarely apply to every situation. Jesus angrily fought the moneychangers in the Temple because they were taking advantage of the poor and innocent. He challenged evil when he expelled the demons* from people who were possessed. He also challenged those who would limit God's love only to people who looked and thought as they did. He clearly was not afraid to fight injustice. When Jesus said to love our enemies, he was teaching us a new way to live with people who are different from us, disagree with us, or oppress us. Jesus wants us to focus on allowing God, not the evil one, to change our relationships. No one wins if our enemies kill or brutalize innocent people.)

- Beginning in Matthew 5:38 Jesus says, "You have heard that it was said, 'An eye for an eye and a tooth for a tooth.' But I say to you...." Is Jesus in open conflict with the words of the Old Testament found in Exodus 21:24-25? (*The Old Testament command to take an "eye for eye, tooth for tooth" was actually an improvement upon the older ways of justice. Prior to that time, people often were killed in retaliation for relatively minor offenses. The "eye for eye" admonition was an attempt to enforce fair justice so that the punishment fit the crime. Jesus, seeking to go even further, demonstrates that God's truth is continually revealed.*)

Watch a nine-minute clip beginning when Antonio arrives at the Iannis home (0:28). End with the scene where Pelagia is in Antonio's room looking tenderly at his family photographs.

- What is your opinion of the way Pelagia and her father greet Captain Corelli? (*Most will understand, especially if they imagine themselves in the same situation. Pelagia's statement, "A brave Italian is a freak of nature," is a knee-jerk reaction to the enemy's presence and is not based on anything she knows about him personally.*)

- During this scene, Pelagia discovers Antonio swinging young Lemoni by the arms. Pelagia sends Lemoni home in a gesture of disapproval. Antonio tells Pelagia, "In times of war, we have to make the most of what innocent pleasures we have." Do you agree with his statement? Why or why not? (*Some would say that times of tragedy serve to highlight the importance of the little things in life. We may suddenly realize that simple pleasures are among our greatest blessings, and we appreciate them more. Corelli provided Pelagia with an important perspective.*)

- When does Pelagia begin to soften toward Corelli? (*After Corelli plays the mandolin the first time, she smiles. The incident provides a glimpse of his humanity. The mandolin is a symbol of love, and all humans possess the ability to love; it is the great bond that ties us together. Pelagia also views him as a family man when she sees the photographs in his room. She begins to let down her guard and to focus on the heart of her enemy instead of the way she has been offended.*)

Watch the scene where Corelli and the Italian soldiers have gathered in the town square to dance and sing for the Cephallonians (0:49). End at the point where Pelagia runs from the square after Antonio plays a mandolin solo (1:04).

- Captain Corelli goes out of his way to maintain civil behavior in the midst of conflict. After his brush with death at the mine explosion, Pelagia says, "You think you can come here and turn my whole world upside down." How does his behavior "turn her world upside down"?
(*When we think of anything as being "upside down," we think of it as being the opposite of what it should be. Pelagia wanted to hate him; instead,*

REEL FAITH 15

# The Real Story Behind *Captain Corelli's Mandolin*

During World War II, Italy, supported by its Axis partner Germany, invaded Greece. The Italian Acqui Division, 11,500 strong, occupied the tiny Greek island of Cephallonia. By all accounts, the Italians got along well with the Cephallonians. When the United States Army took Italy and Mussolini was forced to resign, Italy's new leader commanded his military to refrain from further conflict with the Allied Forces. Like many Italian soldiers who resented Fascism, Acqui Division celebrated and anticipated their homecoming. Their German counterparts, however, continued to fight the war.

Caught between their former Nazi allies and their new truce with the Allied Forces, Acqui Division found themselves in a quandary. If they laid down their guns, as the truce required, should they give them to the Germans, who are no longer their allies? Should they give them to the Greek partisans on Cephallonia? Should they keep them and fight anyone who attacked them?

They decided to join the Greeks against the Nazis. They held out for nine days, but the Germans were too strong, and Acqui Division eventually surrendered after losing at least half their men in the battle. The five thousand or so who surrendered expected to become prisoners of war, but the Nazis had other plans. Since Acqui Division had fought their German "allies," they were labeled as traitors. And traitors could be shot. Few escaped the firing squads.

The world did not know the story of this atrocity until one of the German soldiers present at the firing squads published his diary in a German newspaper in the 1990's. Then in 1995, the best-selling novel *Corelli's Mandolin* spread the story across the world. You can learn more about the truth behind the movie by going to www.awesomestories.com. Click on "flicks."

At the time of publication, all website addresses were correct and operational. Addresses may change in the future.

she felt the opposite emotion. The people expected aggression yet received exactly the opposite. This scene illustrates Jesus' instructions: offer people, in God's name, the opposite of what they would expect. If they expect you to retaliate, turn the other cheek to reveal God's strength in your heart rather than your weakness.)

- After the news that the Allies have landed in Italy reaches Corelli's men, they celebrate. This dumbfounds the German officer, Gunther Webber. Webber and Corelli then have a discussion about "morality." Describe the differences in each man's view of morality. *(Webber sees only the "morality" of power. To him, simple biology dictates that his race is superior and deserving of victory. Corelli's morality, on the other hand, is illustrated by these words: "If I saw a man set upon, I would help him—that is my morality.")*

- Does Corelli's morality remind you of a particular teaching of Jesus? *(The parable of the good Samaritan in Luke 20:29-37 is a perfect reflection of Corelli's morality.)*

Watch the clip beginning where Corelli's commander instructs him to withdraw his battery from the beach and surrender his guns to the Germans (1:18). End when the partisans find and rescue Antonio (1:38).

- As we watch this scene, it is instinctive to root for the Italians. Their cause, after all, is just. They are fighting because they have no other choice, and they are attempting to defend the people of the island. Yet the Italians are slaughtered. With few exceptions, the ones who are not killed in pitched battle are later executed by the Nazi firing squads. Where is God in all of this? *(God is not in the evil of war, nor is God in the bitterness of retaliation. God is found in any act of love or courage that stands apart from these actions. God, therefore, is found in Antonio's rescue and in the courage of his men as they protect the island's inhabitants from harm.)*

- Does Jesus tell us to love the Nazi aggressors in this scene? *(Jesus' command to love our enemies is not open for discussion. Based on Jesus' own example, our responsibility is to defend the weak and the powerless. While it may be easy to love the weak and powerless, humanly speaking it is nearly impossible to love those who would perpetrate such evil. Nevertheless, when we have done all we can to fight the actions of evil people, we are called to reconciliation, not retaliation. Germany today is a staunch ally of the countries it once oppressed. The power of love speaks through history.)*

Watch the scene with Mandras and Pelagia through to the end of the movie (1:47).

🎻 At the beginning of this scene, Mandras tells Pelagia that he rescued Antonio, his rival for her affections. Mandras wanted Pelagia to love him again, but he knew that the love must be real. For that to happen, she must choose between him and Antonio. She chooses Antonio because it is the honest thing to do; she cannot change her true feelings. This raises an important question about love: Can it be created? Jesus, for instance, commands us to love our enemies. However, love often seems to arise unbidden from some source we cannot control. Is it actually possible to love simply because we are instructed to do so? (*Jesus taught about a type of love that does indeed follow a decision to love. It has nothing to do with passion and romance. Instead, it follows a change of heart that results from a decision to follow God. Never doubt the power of God through the indwelling of the Holy Spirit to change your heart's ability to love.*)

 The movie begins and ends with the same humorous situation. Stamatis wants the doctor to replace the pea so he can avoid hearing his wife's constant nagging. How does Dr. Iannis' response reflect Jesus' admonition to love our enemies? (*Dr. Iannis reminds Stamatis that he is also part of the problem. He is focusing only on the way the nagging affects him. Once he begins to focus on his wife, bringing her flowers and being nice to her, love will have a place to grow.*)

## Who Were the Real Pelagia and Antonio?

This movie is based on the celebrated novel *Corelli's Mandolin* written by the British author Louis de Bernieres. Although de Bernieres denies that Antonio and Pelagia are modeled after real people, many have questioned him. There are at least three people whose real-life stories are remarkably similar to the romantic adventures of Antonio and Pelagia.

Italian artillery Captain Amos Pampaloni did, indeed, fall in love with a Cephallonian girl, although she has never been identified. He says an affair never occurred. He and his Acqui Division unit were among those who surrendered to the Nazis. Thinking they were being taken as prisoners of war, they had no idea what was about to happen when they were lined up in a remote area of the island. When the Nazis began confiscating their watches and other possessions, Pampaloni protested, reminding the Germans that POW's were not to be robbed. His protests ignored, Amos took the first shot through the neck. His fellow soldiers fell on top of him as they were gunned down, allowing the wounded Pampaloni to feign death. Like Antonio Corelli, he was discovered by a young boy and rescued by Greek partisans. At this writing Pampaloni still lives in Italy.

Cephallonian Elly Fokas was sixteen when she fell in love with Italian Sergeant Major Walter Gorno. Shy by nature, Walter attracted her attention by playing beautiful songs on his accordion. By the time the murders began, Elly was pregnant. She risked her life hiding Walter first in a well, then in a cemetery, and eventually in her own home. In the novel, Pelagia is beaten severely by her fiancé, Mandras. In real life, Elly was nearly beaten to death by her own brother for harboring the enemy. Walter saved her life, then joined the Greek resistance forces. An Italian priest married the couple shortly before their child was born.

In 1945 Elly, Walter, and their daughter Yolanda made their way to Italy where Elly still lives near her two daughters. (Walter died several years ago.) They frequently visit Cephallonia, considered by many to be a vacationer's paradise.

And how does Corelli's mandolin come into the story? Although Walter Gorno played the accordion, Louis de Bernieres, the novel's author, does indeed play the mandolin.

**REEL FAITH**

# All-American Series: From **American Graffiti** to **American Pie**

# AMERICAN PIE 2

## Background
*American Pie* (1999) is 95 minutes long and is rated R. *American Pie 2* (2001) is 104 minutes long and is rated R. *American Graffiti* (1973) is 110 minutes long and is rated PG.

## Cautions
The *American Pie* movies are rated R for strong sexual content, crude sexual dialogue, and language. *American Graffiti* is rated PG with some language.

## Academy Awards
*American Graffiti* was nominated for several Oscars. **George Lucas** was nominated as Best Director. **Candy Clark** was nominated as Best Actress in a Supporting Role. *American Graffiti* also received nominations for Best Picture, Best Film Editing and Best Writing, Story and Screenplay Based on Factual Material or Material Not Previously Published or Produced.

> "All things are lawful for me," but not all things are beneficial. "All things are lawful for me," but I will not be dominated by anything.
> (I Corinthians 6:12)
>
> Or do you not know that your body is a temple of the Holy Spirit within you, which you have from God, and that you are not your own?
> (I Corinthians 6:19)

# American Pie and American Pie 2

The *American Pie* movies are a conundrum. Despite the fact that they rely on patently offensive and immature sexual humor as their main claim to fame, they have an underlying foundation of maturity in dealing with the sexual transitions encountered by high school seniors and first-year college students. They take their place in a long tradition of coming-of-age movies such as the *Porky's* series and *Losin' It* and can trace their lineage as far back as the beach movies of the early sixties. Something makes us want to watch the uncomfortable antics of boys and girls when they are struggling with the transition into adult sexual relationships.

*American Pie* burst on the scene in 1999 as an unexpected smash summer hit. At the time of this writing, *American Pie 2* was closing in on 150 million dollars at the box office. A lot of people are seeing these movies, and it would be a fair assumption that many of them are Christians. How does a Christian approach films like these? Some would say a Christian should never see a movie like *American Pie*. Others take an "in-the-world-but-not-of-the-world approach," watching the movie for entertainment while understanding that the behaviors expressed by the characters in these movies have little to do with Christian values. One way to teach Christian values is to observe the way the rest of the world approaches sexuality and then formulate a Christian response.

*American Pie* centers on the relationship of four friends who make a pact to lose their virginity by the senior prom. *American Pie 2* follows the same four friends when they come home from college on their first summer vacation. The guys embody familiar stereotypes. Jim, the main character, is the loveable nerd. Oz is the dreamy-eyed jock struggling to express his sensitivity. Kevin is the good looking guy with a longterm relationship, hoping to find a way to take that relationship to the next level. Finch is the artistic intellectual caught between a well-developed mind and underdeveloped social skills. Along for the ride is Steve Stifler, the terminally insensitive party animal who watches his friends' struggles and can't understand why they are so concerned with other peoples' feelings. The girls, too, embody familiar stereotypes. Nadia is the unattainable Eastern European beauty (an exchange student). Heather is the good girl looking for a good guy. Vicky is the longtime girlfriend who wants to hear "I love you" before taking her relationship to the next level. Michelle is the worldly-wise band geek. Stifler's mom is "the older woman."

What makes these movies intriguing, however, is the way they break down stereotypes in regard to young women. The primary focus of the humor in these movies surrounds the humiliation (sexual and otherwise) that the men inflict upon themselves. In contrast to this, the women are strong and self-assured, controlling the relationships with maturity as the men bumble their way through insecurity, insensitivity, and low self-esteem. Whether or not you agree with their choices, the women carefully consider each step in their relationships. And it is, after all, our choices that reflect our values.

## Forming Covenant Groups for Movie Viewing

You would never show films like the *American Pie* movies to a general audience. The content would be deeply offensive to some people. However, you can gather a group of persons who covenant to watch films like the *American Pie* movies in order to react to them from a Christian perspective. If a movie has strong sexual content, crude humor, graphic violence, or even significant language issues, the persons watching the film together should have this covenant relationship to ensure that they are prepared for and able to deal with the content of the film or films they will be watching and discussing.

As Christians we can examine the decisions made by these characters, both male and female. We can consider what the world is saying about sexual values and how we want to respond. We can even put ourselves in the situations the characters face and determine how we would respond or what we would do. We can applaud the good decisions and deplore the bad. We can use what we have learned as Christians as a foundation for good judgment when we consider what the world is offering as an alternative to our values.

To begin the discussion direct the group to create a chart of the important relationships that span both movies. When you are finished, the chart should look like this:

Jim—Nadia
Jim—Michelle
Kevin—Vicky
Oz—Heather
Finch—Stifler's Mom

The two other important characters, Stifler and Jessica, never link up but provide commentary on the other relationships.

## Discussing and Learning

★ How would you describe the relationship between Jim and Nadia? How does it change from the first

**REEL FAITH** 19

movie to the second? *(At first, Nadia is the "unattainable woman" of Jim's dreams. In the first movie he bumbles his chance to be with her. At the beginning of the second movie, she is still the woman he believes he wants, but when he finally gets the chance to be with her, he realizes that he is in love with Michelle.)*

✯ In your mind, what is the difference between infatuation and love? Have you ever been attracted to (or infatuated with) an "unattainable" man or woman?

✯ How would you describe the relationship between Jim and Michelle? How does it change from the first movie to the second? *(In the first movie Jim asks Michelle to the prom as a last resort, but we discover that Michelle is really the one in control. In the second movie she becomes Jim's mentor in the ways of love. By the end of the second movie, Jim realizes that he cares about Michelle and wants to be with her.)*

✯ Michelle is portrayed as a well-adjusted young woman with strong self-esteem and who is comfortable with herself and controls her relationships. Are you like Michelle in any way? Do you know women like Michelle?

✯ How would you describe the relationship between Kevin and Vicky? How does it change from the first movie to the second? *(In the first movie Kevin and Vicky are struggling with the idea of starting their sexual relationship. Kevin puts pressure on Vicky to have sex, and Vicky puts pressure on Kevin to tell her that he loves her. After they initiate their sexual relationship, they conclude that they are not right for each other. In the second movie Vicky has established her independence, and Kevin is struggling with his.)*

✯ At one point Vicky gives Kevin oral sex. Was this an appropriate step in their relationship? If not, when is this appropriate in a relationship?

✯ How would you describe the relationship between Oz and Heather? How does it change from the first movie to the second? *(Oz joins jazz choir so he can start fresh with his relationships and test out a new way of relating to girls—through his sensitivity. By the end of the movie, he and Heather have fallen in love. In the second movie they are struggling to maintain a long-distance relationship.)*

✯ What is the advice that leads Oz to change his way of relating to women? *(When Oz tries to seduce a college-aged girl, she rebuffs him and says, "You don't need to come to a place like Lookout Point and spout off cheese-ball lines to be romantic. Pay attention to a girl; be sensitive to her feelings; remember relationships are reciprocal.")* Does Oz follow this advice?

✯ How would you describe the relationship between Finch and Stifler's mom? How does it change from the first movie to the second? *(In the first movie Finch is left without a date and has a chance encounter with Stifler's mom. In the second movie he has become obsessed with her.)*

✯ Is it appropriate for a middle-aged woman to have a

relationship with a man who has just graduated from high school? How much does the difference in ages between a man and woman matter in relationships?

* With which of these couples or individual struggles do you identify the most? Why?

* Abstinence from sexuality until marriage is taught by the church. How would each of these characters or couples respond if you suggested this alternative to them?

* What are the key factors you would consider before initiating a sexual relationship?

* Read 1 Corinthians 6:9-14. In these verses Paul discusses physical excesses and the need for moderation. How do you feel this Scripture applies to the characters and relationships in the movies? How do they apply to us? *(Emphasize the fact that the key verse in this passage is 1 Corinthians 6:12, Paul's plea for moderation in all things.)*

* Read what Paul has to say next in 1 Corinthians 6:15-20. Discuss Paul's concept of the body as a temple for the Holy Spirit.

* Jim's father provides some of the movie's most humorous moments when he tries to give Jim fatherly advice. Discuss the positive aspects of Jim's relationship with his father. *(Jim's father is absolutely supportive no matter what Jim does to humiliate himself. He reasons with Jim, reassures him, and tells him that he loves him. They are completely open in their discussions, and while it occasionally embarrasses Jim, they can talk about anything. Jim's father makes it clear that he is proud of his son even when he makes silly mistakes.)*

* These films use sexual self-stimulation as a foundation for many of the humorous situations encountered by the characters. Lead an open discussion about sexual self-stimulation. *(Most Christian counselors regard sexual self-stimulation as a natural part of the process of maturing sexually. It is pleasurable. It allows us to experiment with our sexuality and relieve sexual tension. However, we need to follow Paul's advice about moderation. Sexual self-stimulation can become addictive. It can become a coping mechanism to deal with depression and rejection or feelings of alienation and inadequacy. We must always be in touch with our feelings when it comes to sex and sexuality.)*

* Spend some time discussing the films' cavalier attitude toward teen drinking and substance abuse.

# American Graffiti

While you would never show the *American Pie* movies to a general audience, *American Graffiti* allows you to discuss many of the same issues from a PG point of view. *American Graffiti* was filmed in 1973, and it deals with coming-of-age issues in 1962 (when director George Lucas was graduating from high school). Comparing *American Graffiti* to the *American Pie* movies allows us to see how much has changed in

REEL FAITH 21

thirty years. Without a doubt, the primary focus of the *American Pie* movies is sex and sexuality. Relationships and individual struggles are a secondary emphasis.

On the other hand, the primary emphasis of *American Graffiti* is on the key decisions about life and relationships being made by the central characters. Sexual issues are an important part of these decisions, but they are left in the background. While many of the characters wind up in the back seat together, the sexual component is downplayed and left to the audience's imagination.

In 1962 the emphasis was on cruising down the main boulevard with a cool car, hoping to get a girl to jump in and take a ride with you. Instead of outrageous beer bashes, we see the freshman hop. Instead of sexual high jinks we watch innocent pranks: mooning from the car window, tossing a water balloon, yanking down a guy's pants while he's trying to have a conversation with a girl, covering the car in the next lane with shaving cream while it's stopped at a traffic light, and chaining the back axle of the local police car to a pole. *American Graffiti* is about creating fun in small-town America.

Yet while the characters are having fun, they also are making significant, life-changing decisions. Should I get on the plane and leave for college in the morning or should I stay here? Should I make this relationship a lifetime commitment? Should I initiate a sexual relationship? Do I eventually have to realize that I have become an adult? As the characters struggle with decisions, we learn both about them and about ourselves.

As with the *American Pie* movies, begin the discussion by asking the group to create a chart listing important relationships. Finished, the chart should look like this:

Steve—Laurie
Terry—Debbie
Curt—Wendy (his ex)
Curt—The unattainable blonde woman in the white T-bird
John—Carol

## Discussing and Learning

✯ How would you describe the relationship between Steve and Laurie? (*Laurie is the head cheerleader, and Steve is the president of his class. They are an ideal couple. At first Steve suggests that they should see other people since he is heading off to college. Laurie is devastated. By the end of the movie, Steve has chosen to stay at home rather than go away to school.*)

✯ How would you describe the relationship between Terry and Debbie? (*Terry "The Toad" is this movie's nerd. He has Steve's car and picks up Debbie while he's out cruising. She is a wild girl, and Terry will do anything he can to impress her. In the end they like each other, and Terry feels accepted just as he is.*)

✯ How would you describe the relationship between Curt and Wendy? (*Wendy is Curt's "ex." They find they are still attracted to each other, and Wendy becomes one more temptation for Curt to stay home rather than go off to school.*)

✯ Why is Curt infatuated with the blonde in the white T-bird? (*She is that ideal "fantasy woman" that Curt has always imagined but never had a chance with before. He wants to live out his fantasy.*)

✯ What is the relationship between John and Carol? (*Carol is a younger girl and John is tricked into giving her a ride. While he is aggravated at first, they become friends; and he becomes very protective of her.*)

✯ Curt is having second thoughts about going to college. Why do you think he is wavering? Why do you think he decides to go?

✯ Steve decides to stay home rather than go off to college. What are the key factors in his decision to stay?

✯ What part does sexuality play in this movie? How would the film be changed if it had a bigger role?

✯ What are the attitudes toward teen drinking in this movie? How do they differ from those in the *American Pie* movies?

# Video Illustrations

## A River Runs Through It and *Georgia*

Someone has said that we understand universal truths through the particulars. Reconciliation, forgiveness, and acceptance of differences are necessary tasks among differing nations or ethnic populations. They also are important within families who share common genetic traits, cultural heritages, and environmental settings. These two films, *A River Runs Through It* and *Georgia*, portray the mystery of siblings who recognize their differences with one another and struggle to make sense and even peace with them.

### Brothers

*A River Runs Through It*, released in 1992, starred Brad Pitt and was directed by Robert Redford. It is based on a classic short story of the same name written by Norman MacLean. MacLean spent his life as a professor of English at the University of Chicago writing scholarly articles. Yet within him he carries this story of a Presbyterian minister and his two sons. In his retirement, he set out to write this story of his own family history, and he spent two years meticulously recording the

drama of his childhood and young adult years. The movie, a faithful dramatization of MacLean's story, is both visually beautiful and relationally compelling.

The movie begins with these words: "In our family, there was no clear line between religion and fly fishing" (3:40). The viewer is prepared for what is to come: the story of a family, deeply religious, drawn to the mystical practice of fly fishing. The brothers, we soon discover, share a love for fly fishing but seem to be heading in opposite directions. Norman lives the charmed life, preparing for a career as a scholar; Paul leads a troubled life, living in the shadows of the community, just out of reach and sight of his family and its protection.

Read the parable of the prodigal son from Luke 15. Jesus begins with these words, "There was a man who had two sons." Can you hear the lives of Norman and Paul as an echo of this parable?

As the story proceeds, Paul's life becomes more reckless and dangerous; his drinking and gambling expose him

### Background
*A River Runs Through It* is 123 minutes long and is rated PG. *Georgia* is 115 minutes long and is rated R.

### Cautions
*Georgia* is rated R for substance abuse, language, and a sex scene.

### Academy Awards
*A River Runs Through It* won the 1993 Academy Award for Best Cinematography.
*Georgia's* **Mare Winningham** was nominated for Best Actress in a supporting role.

**REEL FAITH** 23

to violence, and he begins to distance himself from his family. One scene portrays a family meal during which the family members struggle to be honest with one another, but they are unable to communicate their worries and anxieties (1:24).

Compare this family meal (where concerns are avoided) with the conversations of the two sisters in *Georgia* (where concerns are confronted directly). Which is more like your own family? Which is most helpful?

Norman has a burden to help his brother Paul, but ultimately Norman is unable to do so. He writes: "In the loneliness of the canyon I knew there were others like me who had brothers they did not understand but wanted to help. We are probably those referred to as 'our brothers' keepers,' possessed of one of the oldest and possibly one of the most futile and certainly one of the most haunting of instincts. It will not let us go" (from *A River Runs Through It* by Norman MacLean, pages 28-29). His character asks along the way, "Why is it that people who need the most help resist it?" (1:33).

The clearest communication within the family happens in the preaching of the father. Late in life and in a sermon, he offers this wisdom: "Those we live with and should know elude us. We can love completely without complete understanding" (1:56). Paul is a handsome, gifted, and determined young man, yet he is as mysterious to those near him as the behavior of a trout is to a master fisherman. Norman reaches out to him, inviting Paul to relocate to Chicago where he will teach, but Paul declines. He is drawn to the magic of the river and to the danger of life closer to home. And so Norman is unable to prevent Paul's self-destruction.

Norman wonders if he is his brother's keeper. Read the story of Cain and Abel in Genesis 4. How are the two stories alike, and how are they different?

## *Sisters*

Released in 1995, *Georgia* depicts two sisters, Sadie (Jennifer Jason Leigh) and Georgia (Mare Winningham). Sadie is disturbed, down on her luck, and driven to succeed as a singer. Her older sister, Georgia, has achieved popularity in that same field, and much of the movie explores the strained relationship between the two sisters who are different in both art and life.

Sadie is addicted to a variety of substances. In one scene Georgia asks, "What are you drinking?" and Sadie responds, "You know me. Whatever is cheap or free." The movie begins and ends with the Stephen Foster folk classic, "Hard

  24 REEL FAITH

Times." If Sadie is an addictive personality, prone to excess, Georgia lives a highly controlled and managed life. Their reunions, which recur throughout the movie, are always a clashing of two cultures. Sadie's culture is what sociologist Tex Sample refers to as "hard living": A friend dies of an overdose, her husband leaves, and her health is declining. Georgia's world is shaped by the desire to create a safe place for herself and her family.

- How would you compare the relationship between the two sisters in *Georgia* to the relationship between the brothers in *A River Runs Through It*?

Georgia is a film about the "hard times" experienced within families. While it would seem that Georgia's world is perfect, a conversation between Sadie and Georgia's husband reveals otherwise. Jake describes some of their difficulty in marriage (18:45): "She slept with somebody, and I slept with somebody; and we hurt each other but we are still together ... she's Georgia and we're going to grow old together."

Georgia, however, is always angry just beneath the surface. Sadie, in contrast, always releases her anger (like a flood!). She is gifted, sings with passion, yet self-destructive. Sadie's personality both draws Georgia toward her (with attempts to help) and repels her.

- Different characters emerge in the film who want to "save" Sadie. Do they help? What do they learn about themselves in the process? How does Sadie resist their efforts?

Late in the movie Sadie and Georgia have a moving conversation: "I watch you, and I listen to you and this gift from God; and I swell up with admiration, and I swear there is no envy; and when I talk to you, I feel there is no one home" (46:30). Sadie is chaos and intensity; Georgia is order and precision. Sadie desires elements of Georgia's life, and Georgia envies Sadie's depth. At the movie's conclusion they have another talk:

SADIE: You never left home ... I must be your worst nightmare.
GEORGIA: I hate the desperation. ...
SADIE: You don't feel anything, any desperation. ... You don't feel pain or suffering.
GEORGIA: That's a gift you mistake for pain. ... Sadie's pain must be fed, kept alive. ... We're all here to serve.

The relationship between Sadie and Georgia is present not only in their conversations, but also when they sing together, whether in a small bar (52:30) or in a large concert setting (they perform a reading of Van Morrison's "Take Me Back" at 1: 07).

REEL FAITH 25

Their styles are totally different: Sadie's vocals are angry and intense while Georgia's are smooth and controlled. Their relationship is always one of struggle.

The sons of Rebekah, Esau and Jacob, struggled in the womb (Genesis 25:22-23). How do you account for the struggles between some brothers and sisters? How do Sadie and Georgia finally learn to live together?

Sadie's heroin addiction leads to her hospitalization, and Georgia comes to her rescue. "I'm really sick," she confesses to her sister. "I really didn't know who else to call." She does improve with treatment. During her institutionalization, she has an unexplained vision of her father. (What do you think it means?) Afterward she lives with Sadie and her family for awhile, during which time Sadie gives birth to her third child. The film seems to point us toward a future reality:

There is a way that leads to death and a way that leads to life.

The movie ends with a performance: Each sister sings Stephen Foster's "Hard Times." Georgia sings the lament before a large crowd; Sadie, returning to a life of addiction, sings in a small club in Portland, screaming the words to anyone who will listen.

In the lives of Norman and Paul and Sadie and Georgia, we encounter core Christian experiences: our temptation to sin, our need for grace, and especially our struggle to comprehend the demands of love toward those closest to us.

For further reflection, find a copy of *Friedman's Fables* by Edwin Friedman (Guilford Press, 1990). Read "The Bridge." This is a classic story about the meaning of help we give to others. It asks these questions: How much responsibility do we have for others? Why are those who are dependent so often calling the shots?

"It is those we live with and love and should know who elude us."
—Norman MacLean, *A River Runs Through It*, page 104

# The Graduate

## Background
*The Graduate* (1967) is 110 minutes long and is rated PG.

## Cautions
Though "restricted" when it was released, *The Graduate* is now considered mild enough to warrant a PG rating. There is a brief moment of nudity but considerable talk related to issues of sexuality, since the primary plot centers around an adulterous affair.

## Awards
**Mike Nichols** won an Oscar for Best Director. **Dustin Hoffman** was nominated for Best Actor. **Anne Bancroft** was nominated for Best Actress. **Katherine Ross** was nominated for Best Supporting Actress. *The Graduate* was also nominated for Best Picture, Best Cinematography, and Best Screenplay (based on material from another medium).

> While we were living in the flesh, our sinful passions, aroused by the law, were at work in our members to bear fruit for death. But now we are discharged from the law, dead to that which held us captive, so that we are slaves not under the old written code but in the new life of the Spirit. ... I do not understand my own actions. For I do not do what I want, but I do the very thing I hate.... But in fact it is no longer I that do it, but sin that dwells within me.... Wretched man that I am! Who will rescue me from this body of death? Thanks be to God through Jesus Christ our Lord!
> (Romans 7:5–6, 15, 17, 24–25)

In *The Graduate*, young Benjamin Braddock graduates from an East Coast college and returns to his parents' home to ponder his future. Besieged by the questions and expectations of those around him, uncertain and confused about what he wants, Ben allows himself to be seduced by Mrs. Robinson, the wife of his father's business partner. Their lifeless and emotionless affair continues throughout the summer. Conceding to his parents' wishes, Ben asks Elaine Robinson (the daughter) out on a date during one of her visits home. This, of course, infuriates her mother. He sets out to drive Elaine away, but instead ends up falling for her. Elaine learns about her mother's and Ben's sexual relationship and returns to school in Berkeley. Ben is determined to marry her, however, and doggedly pursues her throughout her class schedule and routine. Eventually he even follows her to the church on her wedding day.

REEL FAITH 27

Once a prolific letter writer named Paul of Tarsus intended to journey to Spain to start a new church. En route he planned to stop in Rome to visit the newly formed Christian church. Before arriving, though, he wanted that city to know a few things about what he believed. The first eight chapters of Paul's Letter to the Romans deals with this question: How does one find one's own way to self, and how is the self united in relationship to God? Paul believed that the old way wasn't working. The books were full of laws, regulations, expectations, and imperatives put in place by others. Even though such laws seemed like good ideas and ones that should work, Paul said that he found himself acting contrary to his good intentions and living in sinful ways. Paul came to find, he said, that the way to begin to live faithfully is to realize that we are incapable of earning or deserving God's favor. Instead, we can simply accept God's grace in faith and then throw ourselves wholeheartedly into living God's call of love.

*The Graduate* does not invoke God's name, nor does it overtly raise religious themes. Yet protagonist Ben Braddock's spiritual journey in the course of the movie is the same journey Paul recounts in the first part of Romans. Ben is an over-achiever who has done his best to follow the rules and live up to the expectations of his parents and others. He has lived successfully thus far; but for Ben, life feels empty and confusing. He has to wonder if and how he will ever escape his parents' oppression. Contrary to his own values, he begins his relationship with Mrs. Robinson as a form of rebellion—not doing what he wants but instead doing the very thing he hates. In time Ben comes to find that the wages of his activity is the death of his soul. He is called to a life of love in his feelings for Elaine. He repents, turning his back on his former self: his self-absorption, his loveless ways, his non-understanding parents, and his sin. He accepts himself as he is (experiencing grace) and throws himself wholeheartedly into living a life devoted to the one he loves. And so we are encouraged—by both Ben Braddock and the apostle Paul to explore the promise of justification by faith, which is the goal of this study in REEL FAITH.

## Discussing and Learning

- Notice the recurring theme of items being submerged in or viewed through water and list several instances.

(Among others, Benjamin stares at a fish tank while avoiding party guests; Mrs. Robinson tosses his car keys in the tank; Benjamin takes a scuba plunge in the swimming pool; Ben spends countless hours floating in the pool; he avoids his mother's pointed questions while shaving in a steamy bathroom; it's raining when Mrs. Robinson threatens Ben in the car and later when Mr. Robinson confronts him.)

- What are the similarities between these scenes, and what is the significance of the continuing water theme? *(Water is obvious in those scenes where we find Benjamin distancing himself from himself as well as from others, such as being evasive in conversation with his mother. He feels like he's the one in the aquarium with others watching him and waiting to see what he's going to do next.*

### A Baptismal Prayer

Eternal Father: When nothing existed but chaos, you swept across the dark waters and brought forth light. In the days of Noah you saved those on the ark through water. After the flood you set in the clouds a rainbow. When you saw your people as slaves in Egypt, you led them to freedom through the sea. Their children you brought through the Jordan to the land which you promised. In the fullness of time you sent Jesus, nurtured in the water of a womb. He was baptized by John and anointed by your Spirit.

From *United Methodist Book of Worship* ©1992 "Baptismal Covenant I-II" ©1976, 1980, 1985, 1989, 1992 United Methodist Publishing House. Used by permission.

*The car keys drop into the aquarium like bait on a hook. When Benjamin fishes them out, he's reeled in while Mrs. Robinson's plot to seduce him begins. Modeling his scuba equipment is an embarrassment, and he escapes by isolating himself at the bottom of the pool. He's drifting, he says, as he floats aimlessly in the pool. Rain pours during the angry, hurtful conversations with Elaine's parents.)*

- Read the prayer from the *United Methodist Book of Worship* (see above), which names places where water is a powerful presence in the Bible. How does the symbol of water in Scripture differ from the meaning of water in the movie? *(The prayer reflects biblical images of water as creative, saving, healing, and purifying, as well as establishing or restoring relationship with God. Martin Luther once said that religion is like water: It can cleanse and refresh or it can engulf and drown. In the same way that these images share the wide range of water's uses, your group might wish to discuss the ways in which religion can be used to establish relationship with God or to distance persons from one another.)*

- "Just one word. Are you listening? Plastics." For one of Benjamin's parents' friends, that word says everything Ben needs to know about life, about success, about the future. *(And what a word! In other contexts, and this one, too, it could be argued that "plastics" connotes things artificial, cheap, and disingenuous.)*

- If the meaning of life could be reduced to a single word for you, what would that word be? Who speaks that word to you? What is the word your church whispers to you? to your loved ones? to your business or profession? to modern culture or society?

- Party guests identify Ben by his list of accomplishments: "the track star," "the award-winning scholar." Meanwhile, Ben seems embarrassed by this attention and is worried about his future. Do we tend to name and identify others by what they do or by who they are? by what they have achieved or by what concerns them on a deeper level? How can we relate to people on a more personal level rather than the more obvious handles of physical appearance, occupation, and social activity?

- One of the movie's classic lines is when Benjamin says, "Mrs. Robinson, you're trying to seduce me, aren't you?" What may not be entirely clear to Ben is crystal clear to the audience. Identify subtle ways in which Mrs. Robinson leads Benjamin on without naming her obvious intentions; then discuss ways in which Benjamin misses the signals. Also discuss ways in which we may be seduced to sin, whether by subtle temptations that move us closer and closer to wrongdoing or by missing or ignoring obvious signals that warn us of pitfalls.

- Benjamin's seduction is a succession of small steps: a simple ride home, coming inside, looking at a portrait, bringing a purse upstairs. Ask the group to list these steps. Though he is wary of Mrs. Robinson's intentions, Benjamin follows each instruction, not wanting to be impolite or appear foolish. Often our involvement in sin begins with a series of small steps. What character strengths help us to avoid life's snares? At what point can you say to others, "This is a step I won't take," when doing so may seem impolite or appear foolish?

- Why does Benjamin bang his head against the wall? *(His involvement in the affair is contrary to his values. He realizes he's being used. There is regret.)* Why do you think he continues? *(He is frustrated, and perhaps he is punishing himself.)*

- When is Ben able to gain some control in the relationship with Mrs. Robinson? *(When she tells the details about Elaine's conception and having to quit art*

> For surely I know the plans I have for you, says the LORD, plans for your welfare and not for harm, to give you a future with hope.
> —**Jeremiah 29:11**

school. Elaine is Mrs. Robinson's most vulnerable point, because Elaine is the replacement for her own personal dreams.) How does this point of vulnerability and her contempt for Ben combine to create Mrs. Robinson's imperative that Ben not date Elaine? Why is Ben "not good enough" for Elaine?

🎓 Why does Ben treat Elaine the way he does at the beginning of their date? Is there a parallel in human experience that, for some reason, causes us to drive away what we need or would be good for us in deference to something less healthy or wholesome?

🎓 The word *repent* comes from the Old French *repentir*, meaning "to turn around." What motivates Ben's moment of repentance, causing him to turn around and begin to move his life in the opposite direction? Note how he communicates with Elaine in contrast to his lack of communication with her mother.

🎓 The apostle Paul encouraged his readers to "work out your own salvation with fear and trembling" (Philippians 2:12). How does Ben's explanation of his earlier behavior reflect that he's now following Paul's advice? (*Ben realizes that everything he's done, including his relationship with Mrs. Robinson and his rudeness to Elaine, has been a reaction against his parents' wishes and expectations. He is ready to find his own path to adulthood. He knows he has acted self-destructively but now seeks to follow healthy paths.*)

🎓 What does the movie tell us about Carl (Elaine's fiancé) and his idea of love and marriage? How does Ben's vision differ?

🎓 Recall Benjamin's relentless pursuit of Elaine. Francis Thompson, a poet, once wrote of God as "The Hound of Heaven," who follows after us, waiting for us to come around and accept a committed relationship with God. Can you share experiences of God's perseverance?

🎓 What causes Elaine to run away with Ben after all?

🎓 As the movie ends, Elaine and Ben are on a city bus, riding away from an interrupted wedding ceremony. What happens next? What unresolved situations loom ahead? What does the future hold for them? Read Jeremiah 29:11. What hope might the couple find in this passage? What hope do you find for your life? (*Although we do not know what the future holds, we can know that God is the one who holds our future, and God's intention for our lives is good. We can always hold hope in our hearts.*)

## Mini-Trivia:

The youngest man to ever win an Academy Award for Best Actor makes his film debut in *The Graduate*. In fact, he won his Oscar two years before Dustin Hoffman won his first statuette.

1️⃣ Who is the actor?

2️⃣ What was his one (and only) line?

3️⃣ For which movie did he win his Oscar, and how old was he?

4️⃣ For which movies did Dustin Hoffman win his two Best Actor Oscars?

(Answers are below.)

*Trivia answers:* (1) Richard Dreyfuss (2) "Shall I get the cops? I'll get the cops!" (3) *The Goodbye Girl* (1977) at the age of 29 (4) *Kramer vs. Kramer* (1979) and *Rain Man* (1988)

30 REEL FAITH

# Point/Counterpoint:
## From One Shaft to Another

In 1971 I was seventeen years old. I, along with many others, found myself standing in a long line to see a movie that promised to show us something we had never seen before—a Black action hero. The movie was *Shaft*, and while it was criticized for pandering to some stereotypes of Black culture, it transcended so many more. Here was the man "who would risk his life for brother man." He was strong and assertive, the ears and eyes of the street. He was not using or selling drugs. He wasn't a pimp or a numbers runner. He was powerful rather than powerless. He had a healthy distrust of institutions and authority, but he knew how to infiltrate them and turn them to work on his behalf. He was outside the system, but he knew how to play the system to his advantage. He was as comfortable with a white police lieutenant as he was with a young Black radical. He could work a mafia hit man as easily as he could have a conversation with a guy from the neighborhood. He always did what was right rather than what was convenient, regardless of the situation. While he was perfectly capable of using violent means to resolve a problem, he drew his true power from a vast network of relationships with people who knew they could trust him and depend on him to keep his word. John Shaft burst on the scene and immediately entered the pantheon of American icons.

The 1971 version of *Shaft* is usually cited as the best film in a genre of movies that came to be known as "blaxploitation flicks." These movies were designed to capture an audience that had been disregarded and undersold by the movie industry: Black Americans. The movies featured new African American stars and often had all Black casts. Hollywood left no stone unturned. There were Black westerns, Black science fiction fantasies, Black horror movies (who could forget *Blacula*?), and even Black martial arts films. Unfortunately these movies often reinforced some of the worst stereotypes imaginable, and many of them are hard to watch these days without cringing. However, this film genre demonstrated to the industry that other cultures within the larger context of American culture had stories to tell and people who wanted to hear them. These same people were willing to pay money to see them told on the big screen.

The late eighties and nineties produced a group of brilliant young filmmakers who began to tell these stories the way that they should be told. Beginning with Spike Lee's *She's Gotta Have It* in 1986, movies that told African American stories through African American eyes began to

REEL FAITH 31

hit the mainstream theaters. Spike Lee continued to write and direct (*Do the Right Thing*, 1989 and *Malcom X*, 1992). John Singleton gave us *Boyz N the Hood* (1991). Albert and Allen Hughes followed with *Menace II Society* (1993), actor/director Forest Whitaker got into the act with *Waiting to Exhale* (1995), and George Tillman, Jr., gave us *Soul Food* (1997) and *Men of Honor* (2000). What these movies had in common was an attempt to take seriously the experience of African Americans and to say something authentic about the challenges they face in everyday American society. Not all of them were successful on all levels, but they did open the American movie-going public's eyes to a world they had not experienced before.

Now let's consider the remake of *Shaft* directed by John Singleton in 2000. The new *Shaft* was a moderate commercial success (closing in on fifty million dollars at the box office worldwide) but got a lukewarm reception from the critics. Despite the fact that it was a showcase for the considerable talents of Samuel L. Jackson, it seemed to lack the raw power and vitality of its predecessor. The plot centers on a hate crime that results in the death of a young African American male and John Shaft's efforts to bring the perpetrator to justice. This time *Shaft* is a police officer who is "too black for the uniform and too blue for the brothers." He wants to "fight the good fight from the inside" but eventually leaves the police force in order to be able to enforce his own understanding of justice. We have heard this story told many times in a variety of ways featuring the full spectrum of "heroes." There is very little originality or authenticity in this screenplay. The new *Shaft* just doesn't live up to the high expectations demanded by the original *Shaft*.

However, comparing the two versions of *Shaft* from a Christian perspective provides a window into the way American popular culture views an African American action hero and African American culture. We come face-to-face with the stereotypes the two movies promote, as well as the stereotypes they explode. Do the attitudes of these heroes ring true to us? What about the people who surround them? Do they seem real, or are they pale reflections of what they are meant to represent? Has the way the two films define and pursue justice changed over thirty years? Do we agree with this definition of *justice* or do we expect more? What does our reaction to these two films tell us about our own attitudes and ourselves? Do we forgive the excesses of the two films in the name of entertainment? Should we even be making movies like these? The answers to these questions reveal a great deal about the way we view the world.

For more information and cultural commentary about the history of "blaxploitation" films go to *www.blackvoices.com/feature/ blk_history_98/blaxploitation*.

At the time of publication, all website addresses were correct and operational. Addresses may change in the future.

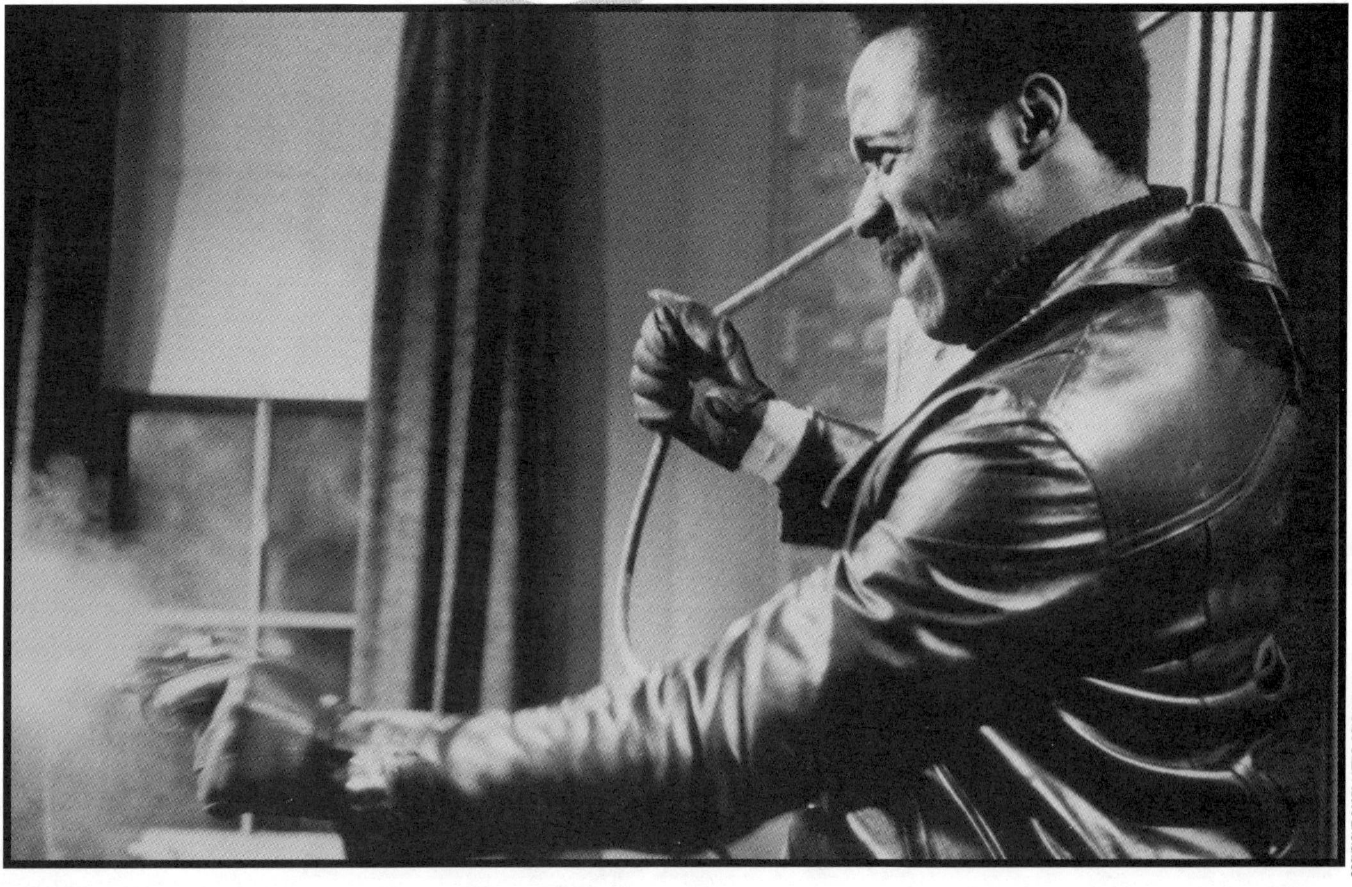

32  REEL FAITH